# BRIGHT SHENG

# THREE CHINESE LOVE SONGS

## for Voice, Viola, and Piano

ED-3923

First Printing: April 1995

# G. SCHIRMER, Inc.

DISTRIBUTED BY

HAL•LEONARD
CORPORATION

7777 W. BLUEMOUND RD. P.O. BOX 13819 MILWAUKEE, WI 53213

# PROGRAM NOTE

*Three Chinese Love Songs* was requested by Seiji Ozawa as one of the commissioned works for the celebration of Leonard Bernstein's 70th birthday at Tanglewood in August, 1988. Prior to this I had just finished a large orchestral work for the New York Chamber Symphony entitled *H'un (Lacerations): In Memoriam 1966–1976,* a work about the "Cultural Revolution" in China. I composed *H'un* around the interval of the minor second instead of using any kind of melody or tune. Since it is about a tragic period in China, the work sounded harsh and dissonant, creating the drama and expressiveness I wished to evoke.

At the same time, the inevitable call for the search of tonality in my writing, though not necessarily in the sense of triads, was increasing daily. I needed to write something quite different. The Tanglewood commission was an opportunity that enabled me to fulfill this need and to explore other compositional ideas. Setting Chinese folk songs seemed natural and appropriate.

*Three Chinese Love Songs* was premiered on August 26th, 1988, on a program entitled "Tributes in Song to Leonard Bernstein" at Tanglewood. The performers were Lisa Saffer, soprano, Burton Fine, viola, and Yehudi Wyner, piano.

—BRIGHT SHENG

## 藍花花　　　　　　　　　I. Blue Flower

Jing Xiarn Xiarn (Na Ge) Lan Xiarn Xiarn,
金 線 線 (那個) 藍 線 線，
Lan (Ge) Ying Ying (Di) Tsai,
藍 (個) 英 英 (的) 彩，
Seng Ha Yi Ge Lan Hua Hua,
生 下 一 個 藍 花 花，
Si Si Di Gnai Si Rarn.
實 實 的 愛 死 人。

Golden thread and blue thread,

They are so pretty,

Just like the beautiful girl,

Her name is Blue Flower.


## 跑馬溜溜的山上　　　II. At the Hillside Where Horses Are Running

Pao Ma (Liu Liu Di) San Sang,
跑馬 (溜 溜的) 山 上，
Yi Duo (Liu Liu Di) Yun (Yo),
一朵 (溜 溜的) 云 (呦)，
Duan Duan (Liu Liu Di) Zao Zai,
端 端 (溜溜的) 照在，
Kang Ding (Liu Liu Di) Tseng (Yo).
康 定 (溜溜的) 城 (呦)。

At the hillside where horses are running,

Right above it is the beautiful cloud,

Which shines over,

The city of Kang-Ding.


Li Jia (Liu Liu Di) Dai Jie,
李家 (溜溜的) 大姐，
Ren Tsai (Liu Liu Di) Hao (Yo),
人 才 (溜 溜的) 好 (呦)，
Zang Jia (Liu Liu Di) Dai Guo,
張 家 (溜溜的) 大 哥，
Kan Sang (Liu Liu Di) Ta (Yo).
看 上 (溜溜的) 她 (呦)。

So pretty is,

The girl from Lee's family,

So much in love with her is,

The boy from Zang's family.


## 小河淌水　　　　　　　III. The Stream Flows

(Ei) Yue Liang Tsu Lai Liang Wang Wang,
(嗳) 月 亮 出 來 亮 汪 汪，
Xiang Qi Wo Di A Guo Zai Sheng San,
想 起我的阿哥在深 山，
Guo Xiang Yue Liang Tain Sang Zou,
哥 象 月 亮 天 上 走，
San Xia Xiao Huo Tang Sui Qing You You.
山 下 小 河 淌水 清 悠 悠，
Yue Liang Tsu Lai Zao Ban Po,
月 亮 出 來 照 半 坡，
Wang Jian Yue Liang Xiang Qi Wo Di A Guo.
望 見月 亮 想 起我的阿哥。
Yi Zeng Qing Feng Tsui Sang Po,
一 陣 清 風 吹 上 坡，
Guo A, Ni Ke Ting Jian A Mei Jiao A Guo?
哥啊，你可聽見阿妹叫阿哥？

The rising moon shines brightly,

It reminds me of my love in the mountains.

Like the moon, you walk in the sky,

As the crystal stream flows down the mountain.

The rising moon shines brightly,

It reminds me of my love in the mountains.

A clear breeze blows up the hill,

My love, do you hear I am calling you?

TRANSLATED BY BRIGHT SHENG

# PRONUNCIATION GUIDE
(Consonants and vowels of the Chinese Phonetic Alphabet and their corresponding International Phonetic Symbols)

| CPA | IPS | | | | | | |
|-----|-----|-----|-----|-----|-----|-----|-----|
| b | ɓ | zh | tʂ | ai | ai | iong | yŋ |
| p | p' | ch | tʂ' | ei | ei | ua | ua |
| m | m | sh | ʂ | ao | au | uo | uə |
| f | f | r | ʐ | ou | əu | uai | uai |
| d | t | | | an | an | ui, uei | uei |
| t | t' | y | j | en | ən | uan | uan |
| n | n | w | w | ang | aŋ | un, uen | uən |
| l | l | | | eng | əŋ | uang | uaŋ |
| g | k | a | a | ong | uŋ | üe | yɛ |
| k | k' | o | o | ia | ia | üan | yan |
| h | x | e | ə | ie | iɛ | ün | yn |
| j | tɕ | i | i | iao | iau | | |
| q | tɕ' | u | u | iu, iou | iəu | | |
| x | ɕ | ü | y | ian | ian | | |
| z | ts | -i | ɹ (ʅ)* | in | in | | |
| c | ts' | êa | ɛ | iang | iaŋ | | |
| s | s | -er | ər | ing | iŋ | | |

* ɹ after zcs, ʅ after zh, ch, sh, and r.

# THREE CHINESE LOVE SONGS

## I. Blue Flower
## 藍花花

Bright Sheng

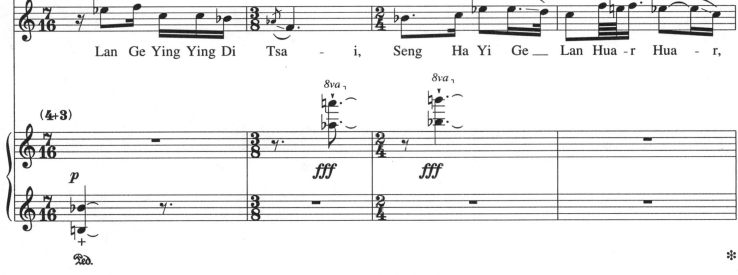

1) + indicates to mute the strings (inside the piano) and play the notes on the keyboard.

2) All grace notes should be played *on* the beat.

3) ⊗ Harmonic overtone, indefinite pitch.

2

\* ⌐ Press down the key(s) silently.

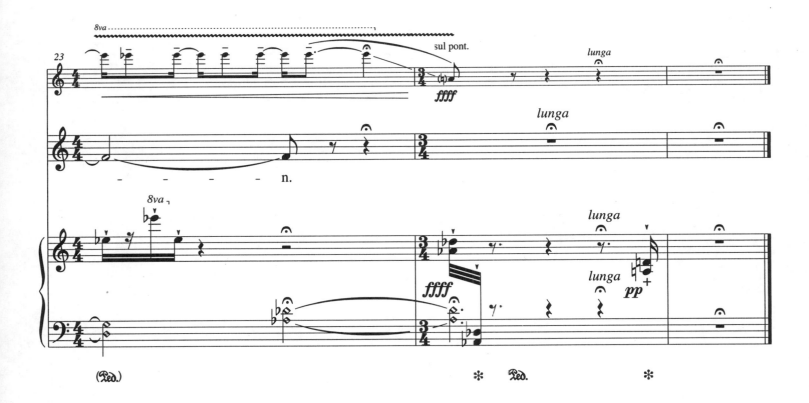

*  〰  Wide vibrato, both above and below the given pitch.

# II. At the Hillside Where Horses Are Running
## 跑馬溜溜的山上

**Viola**

*dedicated to Leonard Bernstein*

# THREE CHINESE LOVE SONGS
## I. Blue Flower

Bright Sheng

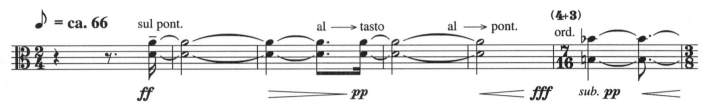

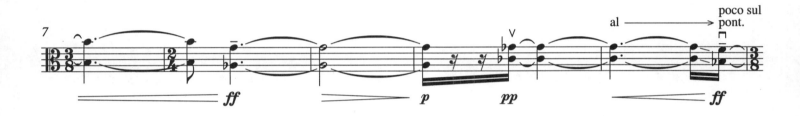

\* 〰 Wide vibrato, both above and below the given pitch.

# II. At the Hillside Where Horses Are Running

# III. The Stream Flows

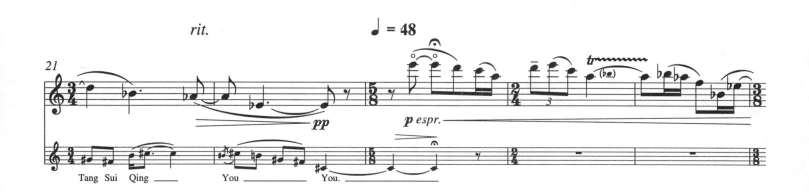

Kang Ding Liu Liu Di Tseng Yo.

Yue Liang _____ Wuan _____ Wuan _ Kang Ding Liu _ Liu Di Tseng Yo. _

# III. The Stream Flows

## 小河淌水

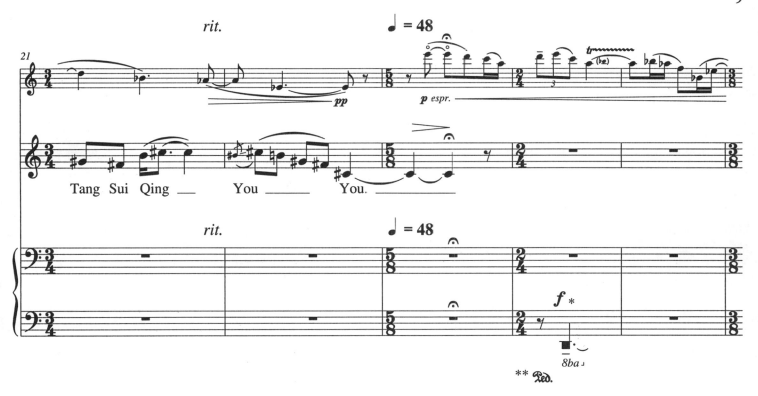

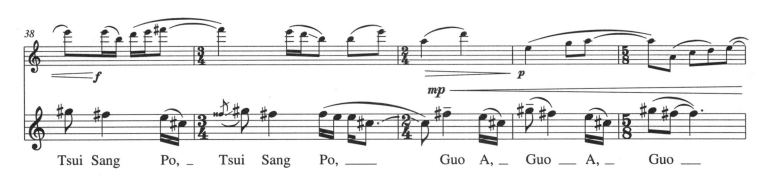

* Use finger tip to tap the string inside the piano.
** From here to the end of the movement the pedal should be held down.

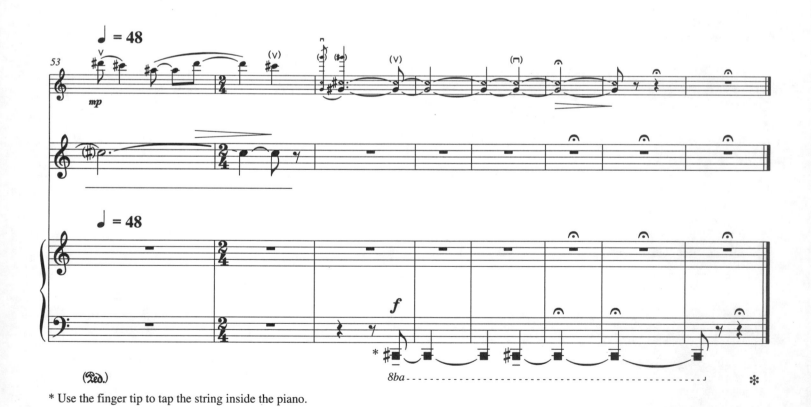

\* Use the finger tip to tap the string inside the piano.